This book is dedicated to those rural Oklahomans who had the foresight and perseverance to transform southeast Oklahoma from the depths of darkness to the splendor of hope and light, and who serve as our reminder that no job is too tough if the cause is just and the people are determined.

Turning the Lights On in Southeast Oklahoma

CHOCTAW ELECTRIC COOPERATIVE
1940–2010

by Herb Matlock

THE DONNING COMPANY PUBLISHERS

Choctaw Electric Cooperative headquarters in Hugo, Oklahoma

Choctaw Electric Cooperative proudly serving Southeast Oklahoma for 70 years

Copyright © 2010 by the Choctaw Electric Cooperative

All rights reserved, including the right to reproduce this work in any form whatsoever without permission in writing from the publisher, except for brief passages in connection with a review. For information, please write:

The Donning Company Publishers
184 Business Park Drive, Suite 206
Virginia Beach, VA 23462

Steve Mull, General Manager
Barbara Buchanan, Office Manager
Heather L. Floyd, Editor
Stephanie Danko, Graphic Designer
Derek Eley, Imaging Artist
Jeanie Akins, Project Research Coordinator
Tonya Hannink, Marketing Specialist
Pamela Engelhard, Marketing Advisor

Ed Williams, Project Director

Library of Congress Cataloging-in-Publication Data

Matlock, Herb, 1932-
  Turning the lights on in southeast Oklahoma : Choctaw Electric Cooperative, 1940-2010 / by Herb Matlock.
    p. cm.
  ISBN 978-1-57864-626-5 (hardcover : alk. paper)
 1. Choctaw Electric Cooperative--History. 2. Electric utilities--Oklahoma--History. I. Title.
  HD9685.U7C476 2010
  334'.6813337932097666--dc22
                                    2010030414

Printed in the United States of America at Walsworth Publishing Company

The Lights of Southeast Oklahoma
by: Brenda Bull Harris

Choctaw Electric Co-op
Keeps the lights on every night
For 70 years they've kept them on
'Cause they know it was right.

McCurtain, Pushmataha and out in Choctaw County too,
To coin a phrase we've heard before
We'll keep the light on here for you.

We turned the lights on in Oklahoma
At least in the southeastern part
You gotta know it wasn't easy,
But our folks have worked real hard.
And we won't stop
Until we know
Your needs have all been met.

The lights in southeastern Oklahoma are on
And we're not done here yet.

The greatest thing on earth is to have the love of God in your heart, and the next greatest thing is to have electricity in your home.

Mission Statement

"Our mission is to embark on a continuous quest to exceed members' expectations of customer service and satisfaction. The cooperative will strive to supply its customers with the highest quality goods at the lowest possible rates, explore and evaluate new technologies, and seek better methods of delivering these services."

Table of Contents

12   Foreword

15   Acknowledgments

16   **CHAPTER ONE**: Flipping the Switch

22   **CHAPTER TWO**: Together We Can

28   **CHAPTER THREE**: The End & The Beginning

34   **CHAPTER FOUR**: In the Spotlight

44   **CHAPTER FIVE**: Reflections of Time

54   **CHAPTER SIX**: Firm Power is Essential

58   **CHAPTER SEVEN**: Decade 2000: Seventy Years of Progress

66   **CHAPTER EIGHT**: The Ice Storms: Testing Times

74   **CHAPTER NINE**: Progressing Toward a Brighter Future

82   **CHAPTER TEN**: Taking the Lead

92   **CHAPTER ELEVEN**: The Choctaw Electric Tradition

98   **What Are Electric Cooperatives?**

101   Electric Cooperative Acronyms & Definitions

102   Rural Electrification Organizational Chart

103   Business Types Compared

     Choctaw Electric Cooperative, 1940–2010

105   Board Managers

106   Board Members, Past & Present

108   Employees, Past & Present

112   **About the Author**

Top row, left to right: Terry Matlock, CEO/general manager; Bob Hodge, vice president/Board of Trustees District C; Henry Baze, Board of Trustees District E; Buddy Anderson, Board of Trustees District D; Mike Bailey, secretary-treasurer/Board of Trustees District B; and Bob Rabon, attorney. Bottom row, left to right: Joe Brisco, Board of Trustees District F; Bob Holley, president/Board of Trustees District G; Rodney Lovitt, Board of Trustees District I; Bill McCain, Board of Trustees District A; and Larry Johnson, Board of Trustees District H.

Foreword

Seventy years ago, in May 1940, a group of Choctaw County residents gathered in Hugo, Oklahoma, and started working on a small idea that turned into something big.

That small idea was to have electric power in their homes and on their farms. This action followed the creation of the Rural Electrification Administration, authorized by President Franklin D. Roosevelt in 1935.

The REA was established as a lending agency, making loans to finance electrical systems that would serve rural areas. When this did not happen, rural residents took matters into their own hands and formed local cooperatives to provide the necessary electrical service.

The Choctaw County group was compelled to establish a local cooperative to serve the needs of the local citizens who had been overlooked by the for-profit electric companies. Choctaw Electric Cooperative, Inc. (CEC) was incorporated in June 1940.

After CEC was incorporated, the founders set out to find enough applicants who wanted electrical service to warrant a federal loan. It took a total of five months to find enough interested applicants to make it feasible to go forward with the loan request. Then, in January 1941, the first loan in the amount of $149,000 was approved.

A contract was awarded to the WALCO Construction Company on March 4, 1941, to build the first section of line consisting of approximately forty-five miles of line serving 250 customers. A little over seven months later, on November 10, 1941, the first electric power was turned on for the Choctaw Electric Cooperative members and we have been keeping the lights on in southeastern Oklahoma ever since.

In December 1941, due to World War II, our efforts to expand Choctaw Electric Cooperative were put on hold as all materials were diverted to the war effort. During this time, we continued serving the forty-five miles of line and

Franklin D. Roosevelt signing the executive order, 1935

EXECUTIVE ORDER

ESTABLISHMENT OF THE RURAL ELECTRIFICATION ADMINISTRATION

By virtue of and pursuant to the authority vested in me under the Emergency Relief Appropriation Act of 1935, approved April 8, 1935 (Public Resolution No. 11, 74th Congress), I hereby establish an agency within the Government to be known as the "Rural Electrification Administration", the head thereof to be known as the Administrator.

I hereby prescribe the following duties and functions of the said Rural Electrification Administration to be exercised and performed by the Administrator thereof to be hereafter appointed:

To initiate, formulate, administer, and supervise a program of approved projects with respect to the generation, transmission, and distribution of electric energy in rural areas.

In the performance of such duties and functions, expenditures are hereby authorized for necessary supplies and equipment; law books and books of reference, directories, periodicals, newspapers and press clippings; travel expenses, including the expense of attendance at meetings when specifically authorized by the Administrator; rental at the seat of Government and elsewhere; purchase, operation and maintenance of passenger-carrying vehicles; printing and binding; and incidental expenses; and I hereby authorize the Administrator to accept and utilize such voluntary and uncompensated services and, with the consent of the State, such State and local officers and employees, and appoint, without regard to the provisions of the civil service laws, such officers and employees, as may be necessary, prescribe their duties and responsibilities and, without regard to the Classification Act of 1923, as amended, fix their compensation: **Provided,** That in so far as practicable, the persons employed under the authority of this Executive Order shall be selected from those receiving relief.

To the extent necessary to carry out the provisions of this Executive Order the Administrator is authorized to acquire, by purchase or by the power of eminent domain, any real property or any interest therein and improve, develop, grant, sell, lease (with or without the privilege of purchasing), or otherwise dispose of any such property or interest therein.

For the administrative expenses of the Rural Electrification Administration there is hereby allocated to the Administration from the appropriation made by the Emergency Relief Appropriation Act of 1935 the sum of $75,000. Allocations will be made hereafter for authorized projects.

The White House,
May 11, 1935

250 customers. However, as soon as the war ended Choctaw Electric began a trend of steady and constant growth and expansion which is still being enjoyed today.

Choctaw Electric presently maintains approximately four thousand miles of line serving Choctaw, McCurtain, and Pushmataha counties as well as portions of Atoka, Bryan, and LeFlore counties and has nearly twenty thousand meters on line.

Choctaw Electric Cooperative provides the membership with a variety of extended services beyond providing electricity to our members. We make available to our members low-interest CEC loans, home energy audits at no charge, career days, office tours, driver safety classes, and educational programs for schools and organizations including Youth Tour and Energy Camp. Choctaw Electric provides Co-op Connection cards to our members that allow discounts on prescription medications as well as other goods and services on a local and national level. The co-op also publishes a monthly newsletter for the purpose of updating members on issues of interest.

We applied for and received a Community Connects grant in 2006 from USDA Rural Development to provide broadband Internet connections for Haworth, Rattan, and Smithville. The goal is to improve public safety, allow residents to pursue educational and economic opportunities, and improve the quality of life in rural areas. Ten computers are available for public use at each site. The broadband service in these areas also connects community centers, volunteer fire departments, police departments, and ambulance service.

In the seventy years since the creation of Choctaw Electric Cooperative, we have grown well beyond the wildest expectations of the founding fathers and our pledge is to continue to exceed the expectations and needs of our membership now and in the future.

Someday all of the people who remember turning the lights on in southeast Oklahoma will be gone. When that day comes I believe the members will still be proud they are part of Choctaw Electric Cooperative because we were not content to merely provide electricity.

Choctaw Electric Cooperative has truly lived up to its commitment to community and has made southeastern Oklahoma a better place to live. I'm looking forward to the next seventy years.

Terry J. Matlock
CEO, Choctaw Electric Cooperative

Acknowledgments

This book would not have been possible without the tireless efforts of a number of people. At the risk of failing to mention some, I want to thank Jia Johnson, Brad Kendrick, Lois Ann Beason, and Jennifer Boling. They went beyond the call of duty digging out old dusty boxes of documents and records. They found old pictures that were used in this publication and also took current photos of people and objects of interest to make this book a memorable pathway for the history of Choctaw Electric Cooperative.

Mr. Bill Grant deserves special recognition for sharing his wealth of historical knowledge about Choctaw Electric Cooperative. We are grateful to everyone who provided pictures, memorabilia, and shared stories and memories that helped make this publication possible.

I especially want to thank the Board of Directors for having the vision to launch this project and the patience to see it through.

CHAPTER ONE

FLIPPING
the Switch

The 1940 novel written by John Steinbeck entitled *The Grapes of Wrath* pretty well describes the living conditions during the late 1930s and early 1940s in America, and in particular Oklahoma, and more specifically southeastern Oklahoma.

It was a dismal time for the United States. The country was coping with the results of the greatest depression in its history. The stock market crash was still spiraling downward, affecting almost every American. Farm families struggled with declining agricultural prices that were dropping to disastrous levels; millions of workers lost their jobs, factories closed, and hunger was widespread. People were destitute with little hope for something better to come along in the future. Faced with disaster, many families migrated to other areas in hope of finding work and a better life.

The drought made the Depression even worse. People depended on their vegetable gardens for most of their food supply and when the grain and hay fields burned up, the gardens went with them. There was barely enough water for livestock and there was very little left for them to forage.

Then the dust storms began. The wind would pick up, and raging dust clouds would roll in without warning, literally blowing away large parts of the region. With nothing to hold down the decimated land, dust storms became a way of life.

Because there was no electricity, rural family life was a daily struggle reminiscent of our pioneer ancestors. Each day began at first light and ended well after dark, using the light of a candle or kerosene lamp. There were many chores to be done: cows to be milked, milk churned by hand, chicken coops cleaned, water

hauled in, wood boxes filled, and since the modern convenience of indoor plumbing was unheard of in those days, daily chores also included cleaning the outhouse.

Wash day was an arduous task. It began with the farmwife building a fire and boiling water in pots. Rub boards were

used to scrub the clothes with homemade lye soap. Clothes were then rinsed in a separate washtub and hung on clotheslines or yard fences to dry. The clothing had to be ironed with heavy "sad" irons heated on the wood stove. Some women fortunate enough would have two or more irons, one in use and one reheating.

In the winter months, wood stoves were used for heating as well as cooking. If the stove went out during the night, one of the first things to do in the morning was to put the kindling on the remaining coals to get the fire going again to warm the house. When this was done, the day's work could begin. First on the list was cooking the

family breakfast. Cooking on a wood stove was a challenge for the farmwife. Dampers had to be adjusted to keep the top burners hot enough to cook whatever food might be in the frying pan or in the kettle without burning the biscuits cooking in the oven.

Bath time was once a week, usually on Saturday. More often than not one tub of bathwater was used for the entire family. Water was carried in from the well and heated on the wood stove or over a fire. As a rule the last person to bathe was the youngest family member and by then had only lukewarm water along with a little grime left behind. Thus the saying, "Don't throw the baby out with the bathwater."

Since kerosene lamps were the only source of light, the lamps were lit at sun down, supper was cooked, and if children were still in school, homework was done. Families gathered in a dimly lit room with only their faces reflected, much like at an outdoor campfire. Rural people lived in darkness.

The standard of living for rural families was much different than that of the city dweller. There was no modern convenience to help relieve the stifling summer heat. There was no running water and no plumbing. Cities, however, had lights, and this would draw many family members away from home. Seeing no future by staying on the farm, many left to seek jobs and a better way of life in the city. Few actually found what they sought after; instead they became part of a problem that President Roosevelt was doing his best to resolve.

President Roosevelt's New Deal sent an assortment of programs across the country in an effort to

pull the nation out of the Great Depression. The Works Project Administration, known as the WPA, was the largest New Deal agency. Construction was the main force of the WPA. Roads, bridges, culverts, parks, small and large dams, schools, and other buildings were built by the WPA. Oklahoma received more WPA-built schools than any other state—a total of 825.

Another New Deal program authorized by President Roosevelt was the Civilian Conservation Corps (CCC). The CCC program was an important part of southeastern Oklahoma. Young men between the ages of eighteen and twenty-eight were eligible to join. They were given food, clothing, shelter, and medical services, were paid thirty dollars a month, and were required to allot twenty-five dollars to their families. Work was needed to replenish trees in burned-out national forests, build paths and trails, and help with the development and conservation of the state's natural resources. The Civilian Conservation Corps was considered an extraordinary program and one of President Roosevelt's best. It gave growing young men work, food, and shelter and an income to help their families. Oklahoma's Roman Nose, Beavers Bend, Robbers Cave, Sulphur, and Osage Hills are a few of the Oklahoma camps built by the CCC that are still in use today.

CHAPTER TWO

TOGETHER
We Can

Realizing the need to have electrical service available to farm families, President Roosevelt created the Rural Electrification Administration (REA) by signing Executive Order No. 7037 on May 11, 1935. The REA was created to make loan funds available for expansion of electrical service to rural areas. The funds would be made available to existing electrical power companies, municipalities, and organized farm groups at a low interest rate and long-term pay-back.

When the REA was created less than 10 percent of the rural areas had electrical service nationwide. Oklahoma had only 2 percent of the rural population receiving electrical service. Why had only a very small percent of our nation's rural areas been able to receive electrical service? Because the commercial power companies could not visualize a profit margin as was being seen in urban areas in which they operated. Consequently, private utilities did not avail themselves to the low-interest loan money and electrical service was not provided to the sparsely populated areas. The few farmers with electricity had to contribute a considerable amount of money toward the cost of service and in most cases it was unaffordable.

The failure of private utilities to bring electricity into rural America left farms and families literally and figuratively in the dark. If the rural population was to

The first annual license issued in July 1940. Choctaw Electric could now begin business transactions for the purpose of bringing electricity to rural southeast Oklahoma.

MINUTES

CHOCTAW ELECTRIC COOPERATIVE, INC.

First Meeting of Board of Trustees

The first meeting of the Board of Trustees of Choctaw Electric Cooperative, Inc. (hereinafter called the "Cooperative"), was held at 203 East Jackson Street, in the City of Hugo, Choctaw County, State of Oklahoma at 7:30 o'clock, P.M., on the 10th day of June, 1940, pursuant to waiver of notice of all the trustees. The meeting was called to order by Jno. A. Bryan, a trustee of the Cooperative, who, upon motion duly made, seconded and unanimously carried, was chosen Chairman of the meeting, and Enoch Needham, also a trustee, was chosen ⸺ thereof.

The Secretary then proceede⸺

and reported that the following

Once Choctaw Electric was incorporated, by laws approved, and the Board of Trustees established, financial records were brought before monthly board meetings for approval.

FINANCIAL AND MEMBERSHIP REPORT JULY 30th TO AUGUST 10th, INCLUSIVE.

We now have a total of 164 paid applications; a gain of 46 since the last meeting of the Board of Trustees. Approximately 104 of these paid applications are situated along the route of the proposed first section. We have applications from twenty-one schools which may be paid sometime in September. Eleven of these are on the first section.

The following is a financial statement from the time of the last meeting to date.

RECEIPTS

Balance forward National Bank of Commerce July 30, 1940	$157.92
44 paid memberships at $5.00 each	220.00
post dated checks redeemed by M. H. Moomaw	25.00
Refund on light meter deposit	..34
Total	$403.26

DISBURSEMENTS

H. H. Moomaw, survey work	63.00
Russell Haynes, survey work	48.80
Carrol Needham, survey work	29.08
Total	140.88
Balance forward National Bank of Commerce August 10, 1940	262.38
Total	$403.26

We owe our survey workers the following amounts:

Member List

Archy School District #44
Atlas Baptist Church
Atlas School
Herbert Alder
Roy Aubrey
Carl Ashmore
Leslie Ashmore
Pearl Armstrong
O. G. Adams
H. E. Akard
Mae Akard
E. B. Atterbury
W. L. Antwine
L. A. Blackman
Charles A. Bolin
Bethel Methodist Church
Homer Burgess
Jno. A. Bryan
W. M. Bass
Roy Booker
J. H. Boone
J. H. Bright
Robert Bates
Ed Beaty
E. L. Blackwell
Bailey Baker
J. W. Brewer
E. E. Bussell
George Booker
J. W. Brown
J. S. Bugg
W. B. Cooley
D. F. Coley
O. D. Cochran
I. H. Cody
Homer Collins
Charles Cross
S. L. Cowley
Henry Cain
J. O. Cobb
Pauline Cobb
Horace Crane
J. C. Collison
Church of Christ at Frogville
Church of God at Grant
W. A. Carley
S. B. Cocke
Eunice Blackard *(Cochran)*
H. A. Cochran
George E. Conrad

O. F. Davis
W. A. Diffie
C. E. Dudley
Eastern Star Church
Grant Edwards
E. F. Ellis
B. F. Ervin
B. O. Floyd
L. W. Frazier – *(J. W.)*
Forest Home School
Susan Frazier – *(J. W.)*
Forney Baptist Church
Oscar Frazier
Forney School
W. A. Finney
Frogville School District #23
A. T. Farr
T. R. Floyd
Mattie Frederick
J. M. Goin
Belle Granthum
W. E. Gorbett – *Trnsf. to J. E. Gardner*
Ray Grant
O. B. Glass
S. E. Grant
Mrs. R. R. Goodman
Roy Harrison
E. M. Horne – *(Ellis M.)*
R. J. Haynes Sr.
R. J. Haynes Jr.
Bill Horton – *(W. L.)*
Frank Hendrick
Newman Helm
Bud Hooker
R. L. Harwell
Frank Hedge
W. B. Hartgraves
Ernest P. Holman
M. T. Hill
G. C. Irwin
J. L. Iglehart
Roy Johnson
H. H. Jones
Johney A. Jeffrey
Ed Hulen
Roy Jackson
Simon Jackson
R. L. Kuhne
Earle Labor
L. K. Johnson

After Choctaw Electric was established, it was necessary to secure a sufficient number of applicants who wanted electric service in order to make a loan application for funds to build the first project. This took a total of five months. Then, on January 25, 1941, the first loan in the amount of $149,000 was approved. Names were submitted to the Board of Trustees, approved, and recorded in the minutes at the monthly board meetings.

receive electrical service, they would have to make it happen by their own efforts. The REA loans furnished the incentive for rural electric cooperatives to form. Forming an electric cooperative was not an easy task. The Rural Electrification Administration wanted to help, but they needed to make sure that projects financed were feasible and could pay back the money that was borrowed.

In 1940, a small but determined group of local men decided to organize an electric cooperative to serve the rural communities of southeast Oklahoma. No doubt, rural electric cooperatives started out very much a dream to a lot of area farmers. Maybe a few years down the road they too would be able to enjoy the benefits of electricity as their city counterparts had. However, in order to realize this goal, hard work and commitment would be necessary.

The first recorded activity is dated June 10, 1940, at 203 East Jackson Street in Hugo. A group of seven men met and the first meeting of Choctaw Electric Cooperative was called to order. The seven original incorporators were also the first Board of Trustees: Ray Grant, Enoch Needham, S. M. Dancer, B. E. Nobles, Jon A. Bryan, Jim Miller, and Paul E. Mollenkopf. These seven co-op trustees also became the first members of Choctaw Electric Cooperative, each paying a five-dollar membership fee.

> If you lived in rural America during the 1940s, you will remember the day the lights came on. The day we got electricity at our house a friend and I had gone fishing down at the river. We returned after dark and I remember walking into my room and pulling the string to turn on the light. After we got electricity, we added two appliances, an electric icebox and an electric washing machine.
>
> A man in a country church said, "The greatest thing was to have the love of God in your heart and the next greatest thing was to have electricity in your home." This phrase has been repeated many times. With the coming of electricity, rural America was changed forever.
>
> Bill McCain
> *Choctaw Electric Board*
> *of Trustees*

This organizational meeting included adoption of bylaws, a report that articles of incorporation had been executed and filed with the secretary of state of the state of Oklahoma, and other business necessary to the completion and organization of the cooperative.

Choctaw Electric opened for business in March 1941. Headquarters were at 116 North Second Street. The building was provided rent-free for up to six months by the Chamber of Commerce to encourage location in Hugo.

Pictured above is an early CEC Board of Trustees and attorney.

When all action was completed and the meeting was adjourned, electricity for rural southeast Oklahoma had become a reality.

On July 30, 1940, the first annual license was issued by the state of Oklahoma authorizing Choctaw Electric Cooperative to transact business as an electric cooperative.

With the first license in our hands, we were off and running, providing electric power and turning the lights on in southeast Oklahoma for the first time in the history of the state.

CHAPTER TWO: TOGETHER We Can   27

CHAPTER THREE

The
END
&
The
BEGINNING

70 years

PEOPLE - POWER - PROGRESS

Despite Choctaw Electric Cooperative's solid structure of today, many problems were faced in its early years due to war interruptions that could have easily destroyed its hope. It took perseverance, foresight, and dedication to the ultimate objective on the part of the early organization to bring it into being and keep it headed in the right direction.

Growth of rural electric expansion was slow until Congress enacted the Pace Act in 1944 which set interest rates at 2 percent and loan repayments could be made over thirty-four years. Rural electric cooperatives all over the country pledged to Congress that they would provide electrical service to all the people in their area. Choctaw Electric Cooperative has strived to fulfill this obligation and has service available to the people in the areas we serve.

With the end of the war in 1945 and the beginning of the economic boom that followed, Choctaw Electric Cooperative began a period of modest growth; great effort was put forth to serve all who wanted electrical service. By 1947, we were serving over one thousand members in Choctaw, Pushmataha, and McCurtain counties. But like other cooperatives, growth was a relative term. Revenue from the

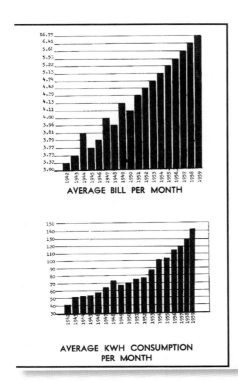
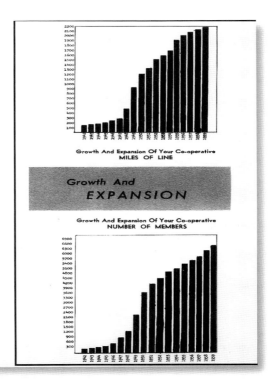

This graph indicates the growth and expansion of Choctaw Electric Cooperative in its first twenty years of serving rural southeast Oklahoma.

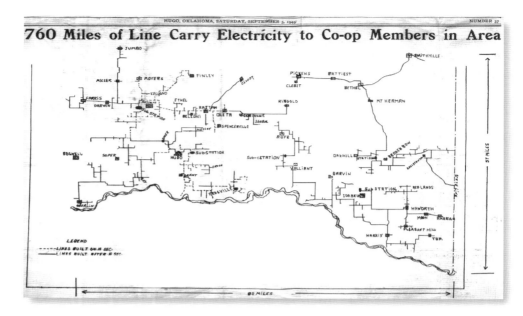

As demand for electricity grew in rural southeast Oklahoma, so did our service area. The map indicates line growth and expansion of Choctaw Electric serving Choctaw, McCurtain, and Pushmataha counties.

Registration at Choctaw Electric's annual membership meetings was rather uneventful for the first few years until 1947. In celebration of five years of service in three counties, Congressman Carl Albert was the principal speaker. Hugo merchants advertised the event and featured a number of items as Choctaw Electric Day specials. That year, over one thousand were in attendance at the annual meeting held at Ansley Park. This photo is of unidentified CEC employees in an unknown year at an annual membership meeting.

forty-five miles of line and the 250 customers we had built and maintained prior to the war was about to change for the better.

Being small is not all bad. It meant that Choctaw Electric Cooperative employees got to know their customers on a first-name basis. Being a smaller electric cooperative also meant that fewer people would share in the cost of installing lines and receiving electrical service. The pioneer fathers of Choctaw Electric Cooperative were dedicated to providing electricity at affordable prices with quality service to rural families.

The early days of rural electrification are all unique but similar. The cooperative's Board of Trustees put emphasis on getting the most out of each dollar of revenue received. Members read their own meters, employees performed several different jobs, and arrangements were made with telephone companies to share the cost of poles. Revenue went straight back into the cooperative's operation.

Little by little, Choctaw Electric Cooperative grew. At the 1950 annual meeting, Choctaw Electric Cooperative had 3,838 members connected along 1,231 miles of line.

Installation of poles was not an easy task. Hand-diggers and spades proved to be challenging, but dedicated and hardworking Choctaw Electric employees labored to bring electricity to farms and rural communities in southeast Oklahoma.

The rural population began to increase. With electricity came a higher standard of living for rural families. Farmers were able to increase their family's income of four hundred dollars annually in 1940 to $2,400 from the sale of livestock and crops. In addition, more city folks were moving to the country because rural areas now had access to telephone service, better roads, and low-cost electricity.

A 1949 CEC payroll check for Mr. Lentz. He worked forty hours at seventy cents per hour and eighteen hours of overtime at $1.05 per hour. *Photo and caption courtesy of Stella B Lentz-Miller and Mark Lentz, son of Joe Lent*

An ad from the September 1, 1949 edition of *The Southeast Oklahoman* newspaper announcing the annual membership meeting. Our annual membership meetings have always been family-oriented and we have continued that tradition throughout our seventy-year history.

EMPLOYEES at the Choctaw Electric Cooperative offices in Hugo are pictured here with Jack Gambrell, co-op manager. Seated, from left, are Winema Marbut, secrtary and news letter editor; Mickie Braudrick, loan clerk; Johnnie Rosenthal, secretary-billing clerk, and Nettie Hendley, billing supervisor. Standing, from left, are Vernon Aulgur, materials and storekeeper; Billy Frazier, bookkeeper; Hershel Simpson, loan advisor, Robert Parnell, meter maintenance; Leon Bates, office manager, and Gambrell. Not present when the picture was taken were Vance Womack, electrification advisor; Sebe Rice, work order clerk and dispatcher, Willie Mae Nelms, billing clerk; Mary Gilbreth, cashier-receptionist, and J. A. Phorney, meter maintenance.

Electricity came to our house a few years later than it did to Rattan. We lived two miles south of Rattan and a half-mile east of what is now Highway 93. It was a two-rut wagon road then. I walked through the woods then to catch the school bus. This was 1944. Throughout school, my lessons were done by a coal oil lamp. I graduated high school in 1950.

About 1957 I was living in west Texas when I got a letter from home saying we finally had electricity at home. The house had been wired with one light hanging in the front room and one outlet on the wall. The old wooden icebox was replaced with an electric refrigerator. Our light bill was about four dollars a month.

Fifty years later, we have two refrigerators, a deep freeze, an electric stovetop, a shop, a welder, three TVs, a computer, and numerous other electric devices. My electric bill is still less than my phone and two cell phones.

I am very proud of Choctaw Electric and proud to have been a part of it as a board member for the last several years. We hope that we can continue to serve our members in the best possible way in the future.

Henry Baze
Choctaw Electric Board of Trustees

Joe and Stella Lentz. Mr. Lentz was employed by Choctaw Electric in January or February 1947. He was transferred from Hugo to Idabel in the summer of 1948. Mr. Lentz worked for CEC until he moved to Corpus Christi, Texas, in 1953, where he remained until his death in January 1971. *Photo and caption courtesy of Stella B. Lentz-Miller and Mark Lentz, son of Joe Lentz.*

With the backlog of new service applications completed, Choctaw Electric was now faced with the problem of its new growth demand. Outpacing the ability of the power supplier to service the load with dependable power, the cooperative continued to expand and upgrade facilities. Choctaw Electric presently provides the finest state-of-the-art electrical service to almost twenty thousand customers and four thousand miles of line with a total investment of more than ninety million dollars. We are keeping the lights on in southeast Oklahoma.

CHAPTER FOUR

In the
SPOTLIGHT

When the original founder of the cooperative met in the district courtroom in Hugo on May 8, 1940, to discuss the possibility of organizing a rural electric co-op, little did they realize the far-reaching effect their efforts would have on the social and economic welfare of the rural areas.

The meeting confirmed the need to create the cooperative and for development of the articles of incorporation and bylaws. By the time the next meeting was held on June 8, 1940, a charter for the new electric cooperative, known as Choctaw Electric Cooperative, had been issued by the secretary of state.

After organization of the co-op, it was necessary that a sufficient number of members request to have electrical service. After exhaustive efforts by the original group, 250 people applied for electrical service and a loan request for $145,000 was submitted to the Rural Electrification Administration for installation of 150 miles of rural electric lines.

On January 25, 1941, the requested loan was approved. Action was undertaken to secure right-of-ways and a contract was awarded to Walco Construction Company on March 4, 1941, to build the first section of line. Choctaw Electric Cooperative turned the lights on in southeast Oklahoma for the first time on November 10, 1941.

The Grant family has been involved in Choctaw Electric Cooperative's history from the very beginning. Ray Grant helped organize the cooperative in 1940 and even donated the land for the first substation. He was also one of the first members of the cooperative. Although power lines were built, the voltage needed to be checked and because Mr. Grant lived near the substation, a monitor was installed in

First home to receive electricity from Choctaw Electric Cooperative. *Photo provided by Bill Grant.*

his home. After a few days, electrical service was provided to those members along the first section of electric lines. A vision shared by a small group of men had come to fruition and would benefit all of us in the years to come.

In a recent interview with Ray Grant's son, Bill stated, "Bringing electricity into rural areas was perhaps the most important thing that happened in his lifetime." Ray Grant passed away in July 1977 after serving the co-op for thirty-seven years. He was replaced on the board by his son, Bill, who served for another five years until 1982.

While the next section of lines was being worked up for submission to the Rural Electrification Administration, World War II began. All materials needed were directed to the war effort. Construction came to a virtual standstill for most electric cooperatives. Choctaw Electric Cooperative had to concentrate on maintaining its forty-five miles of line and 250 customers until the war ended. Bill Grant recounted that "lots of folks had their dues paid and morale dropped considerably. They thought that they would never receive electricity."

Charter members Ray Grant, Leon Bates, and Jon Bryant visit while cooperative members arrive to celebrate yet another successful Choctaw Electric annual meeting.

In 1944, before the war ended, the federal government recognized the need for electrical service to the rural people in order to increase production of agriculture products, and make available materials that were not accessible due to the war effort. Now that material was obtainable, expansion of electrical service could resume. Choctaw Electric Cooperative had applied and was approved for an additional loan of fifty thousand dollars.

Following World War II, it was no longer necessary to seek customers. Everyone wanted electrical service. Large groups of people came into the office demanding it. The cooperative would take their application and

A 1982 photo of Bill Grant, who followed in the steps of his father, Ray Grant, and served a number of years on the Board of Trustees. He continues to be an avid member of Choctaw Electric Cooperative and an ambassador promoting tourism in southeast Oklahoma. Bill Grant's Early Bird Bluegrass Festival is an annual event held in Hugo toward the end of March.

Number **627**

Choctaw Electric Cooperative, Inc.

MEMBERSHIP

Certificate

THIS CERTIFIES THAT A MEMBERSHIP IN

Choctaw Electric Cooperative, Inc.

hereinafter called the "Cooperative"

IS HELD BY_____ TOOTER SAVAGE, FINLEY, OKLA. _____

IN WITNESS WHEREOF *the Cooperative has caused this certificate to be signed by its President and Secretary and its corporate seal to be hereunto affixed this_____ day of_____, 19__*

CORPORATE SEAL.

Jno. A. Bryan, President.

Gray Grant, Secretary.

R∮A CO-OP

(Conditions of membership stated on back)

THE SOUTHEAST OKLAHOMAN, HUGO, OKLAHOMA, SEPTEMBER 1, 1949

HEADQUARTERS of the Choctaw Electric Cooperative is in the Drush building at 312 East Jackson street, Hugo, to which the growth of the cooperative a year ago necessitated moving.

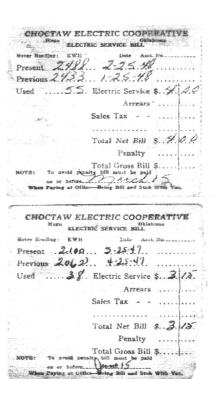

One of the first electric service bills. Members read and recorded their own meter readings and kilowatt usage. In most instances, the kilowatt usage was limited to lights only, unless you were fortunate enough to have a refrigerator and an electric stove. *Electric service bill courtesy of Mrs. W. C. Savage, Finley, OK.*

provide them with service as quickly as funds were available to satisfy the demand. In 1949, the cooperative had invested its first million dollars in electric plants. Bill Grant told us, "It was then that rural America really reaped the harvest of electricity. In my estimation, that was what made the United States the most productive country in the world."

Bill Grant, most recognized for his achievements in bluegrass music, knows a lot of stories about the history of Choctaw Electric Cooperative. He recently recalled the ice storm that happened in 1951. This storm was just as devastating as the 2000 ice storm with the exception that modern equipment was not available to the crews to restore power and repair the lines. In January 1951, temperatures fell below zero in Hugo and Fort Towson. Bill Grant said, "The miles of line and the number of homes weren't as big then. Had it been, the ice storm would have been compared with the damage in 2000." He continued, "Power lines had so much ice on them that they nearly touched the ground, and so heavy with ice that poles would break." For poles that did not break, "co-op employees used axes to chop off the ice. When enough ice was chopped off, the lines would jump back up and just sing."

The vision, dedication, and determination of people like the few men who founded Choctaw Electric have an everlasting impact on all of our lives. An example of this can be seen in the following letter, published November 1998 in the monthly newsletter, *Inside Your Co-op*:

> Southeast Oklahoma has made a lot of progress since the good old days when we had to carry milk to the spring to keep it cool in the summer. While growing up, that was always one of my jobs.
>
> Since rural electrification came to our area, our way of life changed for the better. Affordable electric energy has brought modern conveniences, progress to agriculture, and allowed industry to bring jobs to our area.
>
> The Board of Trustees and management of the co-op encourage the wise use of electricity to keep it always affordable.
>
> Buddy Anderson
> *Choctaw Electric Board*
> *of Trustees*

> . . . My thoughts have traveled back to 1945 when I, a born, reared, and educated "city girl," came to rural Pushmataha County. My husband, Gordon, and I married in 1942 in Kansas City, Missouri . . . He was a native

There have been two destructive ice storms in Choctaw Electric Cooperative's history that devastated the CEC system. Poles and trees snapped like matchsticks, causing major outages throughout the system, leaving members in the dark. *Photos donated by Bill Grant.*

of this country and wanted to return here after the close of the war. I, being very naïve as well as ignorant of the rigors of rural living, told him "I will live anywhere there is electricity."

Gordon was discharged from the service in Lincoln, Nebraska, in December 1945. We packed our belongings in our 1937 Ford Coup and headed for Moyers, Oklahoma, to begin the rest of our lives together. . . . Moyers was apparently one of the places that received electricity before the beginning of World War II. Electricity consisted of a long drop cord hanging from the center of the ceiling of each room with a bare bulb attached. Wall outlets were limited to one or two in each room.

. . . No wall switches, no central heat, no running water, no inside plumbing; [these] were only a few things I had always taken for granted. But there WAS electricity.

Learning to use a wood cook stove was a great challenge. Forgetting to add wood would bring cooking to a stop and the oven to cool, causing baking failures. When I complained, often with tears, Gordon would remind me, "But honey, we have electricity."

. . . An eight-inch Emerson electric fan was truly a treasure and served first to make our baby daughter comfortable through her first Oklahoma summer. That little fan was a family member for many years, and moved from place to place in the house wherever a little air was needed to be circulated. Today, when I turn on the air conditioner and enjoy the refreshing cool air, I still remember the little Emerson fan. I take for granted tossing clothes in the washer, turning a knob and walking away while clothes are washed. However, I do not forget heating water in a big black iron pot in the back yard and carrying it to the wringer washer to do the weekly families [sic] wash. When there is an abundance of warm water for bath or shower I remember the many buckets of water carried into the house for bathing in front of a wood stove. When I want a quick meal, or a cup of tea, or a snack of popcorn, the microwave oven is the answer, but I still recall the wood cook stove . . .

I am glad there was electricity then and glad I have the opportunity to see the use of electricity expand to make life more comfortable and easier than it was in 1945. In reality, I would not go back to then, but I would not trade experiences and challenges of the past 52 years in Moyers, where there WAS electricity.

Thank you, Choctaw Electric, for being there!

Gretchen M. Fredrick

CHAPTER FOUR: In the SPOTLIGHT   43

CHAPTER FIVE

REFLECTION
of Time

I ke Simpson was one of our original loyal and dedicated employees who helped make Choctaw Electric Cooperative the great organization that it is today. Ike recalled his early days in a past issue of *CEC Inside Lines*.

"The Days of Dynamite and One Rubber Glove": Simpson Recalls CEC History
by Mary Wolf

Ike Simpson dodged artillery and rifle fire during World War II, trekked with the 45th Infantry Division across the mountains of Sicily and pitched a fast ball for minor league baseball teams in Arkansas, Texas and Louisiana. Such experiences shaped him for the trek of a lifetime, digging holes, clearing brush and stringing the first power line that brought light and a better quality of life to southeast Oklahoma.

At 86 years of age, the Hugo resident recalls his younger days with quiet humor and due respect for the early hardships. Hired by Choctaw Electric in 1946, his first job included clearing right of way[s] and digging holes for high line poles with a shovel. "Back then we didn't have hole diggers and we did it by hand the hard way. It was rough but I was young and I could take it," he said.

Ike said CEC used an old army truck to carry rolls of amerductor across Pushmataha, Choctaw and McCurtain counties. "And we hired mules to pull the line across the country," he said. Back then most roads weren't paved. "When it rained we got stuck—a lot," he said.

Ike earned a whopping 35 cents an hour as his starting wage. At the time CEC employed 18 people and supplies were limited. "We only had one rubber safety glove for handling

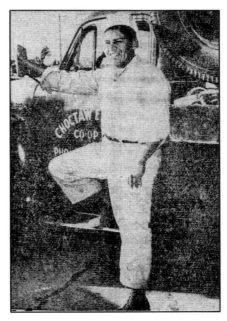

IKE SIMPSON, a lineman for Choctaw Electric Cooperative, is shown in the above picture standing by one of the co-op's trucks. Simpson has been with the co-op since October, 1946. (Staff Photo)

7200-volt line and the foreman carried it. The rest of us wore leather work gloves," he said. "And we only had two or three hot sticks to connect and disconnect lines, but it was a start."

Ike graduated from the right of way crew to journeyman lineman. Later he became an area serviceman, a position he held until retiring from CEC in 1987. In the capacity of serviceman he and one other employee, Monroe Shepard, were the only two employed by Choctaw Electric at that time. They were required to travel over the entire service area. Working for seven different general managers, Ike witnessed the co-op's steady growth and the improvements in technology, equipment and especially safety practices.

Years ago it was common for co-ops to use dynamite to blast through bedrock to erect high line poles. "We'd drill down so many feet and insert a stick of dynamite to loosen the rock," he said. On March 27, 1948, Ike was directly above a hole when the dynamite exploded prematurely. "I thought I'd lost my whole face," he said. Instead he lost one eye and nearly lost sight in the other. In a second close call a pole broke and Ike rode it down to the ground. He broke both hands when it fell.

Hired by Choctaw Electric in 1946, Ike Simpson's first job included clearing right-of-ways and digging holes for high line poles with a shovel. Ike earned a whopping thirty-five cents an hour as his starting wage. He was one of our original loyal and dedicated employees who helped make Choctaw Electric Cooperative the great organization that it is today. Ike retired in 1987. He continues to stay active playing golf and spending time with his children and grandchildren. Ike also enjoys relaxing at home with his wife Bobbie.

From time to time, Ike stops by the co-op. "I go by to see the boys. Nowadays, they work out of bucket trucks and use digger trucks. I tell them they've got it easy and they laugh. They don't know—"

Vance Womack was one of the first to be hired at Choctaw Electric in 1941. He served the co-op for thirty-five years before retiring in 1976. Vance has since passed

FOUR MEMBERS of the Choctaw Electric Cooperative outside crew are shown above. In front are Odell Popchoke, left, a lineman in charge, and James Clark, a lineman. Standing are Farney Harmon, left, line superintendent, and Elmer Hinsley, a lineman in charge. Popchoke has been with the co-op since September, 1946 —Clark since December, 1952, Harmon since May, 1956, and Hinsley since October, 1946. (Staff Photo)

HERE ARE four more members of the Choctaw Electric Cooperative outside crew. In front are Lloyd Wilkins, left, a lineman and Berry Roan, Jr., also a lineman. In back are Andy Wilkins, left, a groundman and Sam Linkswiler, also a groundman. Lloyd Wilkins has been with the co-op since July, 1955, Roan since April, 1953, Andy Wilkins since March, 1956, and Linkswiler since July, 1955. (Staff Photo)

Prior to the current means of right-of-way clearing using gasoline-powered chainsaws, chippers, and bucket trucks in addition to many other modern methods, the only equipment available to the first right-of-way crews were sickles, cross-cut saws, slings, and sometimes assistance from Choctaw Electric members. Right-of-way clearing was grueling physical labor and many employees began their tenure with Choctaw Electric as part of a right-of-way crew.

Vance Womack was one of the first to be hired at Choctaw Electric in 1941. He served the co-op for thirty-five years before retiring in 1976. With few employees in those early days, Vance's duties were many, and included everything from organizing town meetings for enlisting new members to negotiating for right-of-way easements. Vance formed many friendships while working at the co-op. He was always getting a wave or a friendly greeting. They may not have remembered Vance's name, but they recognized him as a Choctaw Electric employee.

on; early employees like Vance Womack set the standard. In the May 1998 issue of *Inside Your Co-op*, Vance spoke of the time before rural communities banded together to form Choctaw Electric and the importance of quality service.

"I was working at a hardware store at the time," said Vance, "and I asked the nearest electric server to bring power to our home in Antlers. They drove out, took one look around and then turned right around and left. They didn't even stop by to say 'No,' I had to call to find out they wouldn't serve us."

It wasn't long after that the cooperative was formed, and Vance hired on. "There wasn't any line strung yet," said Vance. In fact, the general manager hired out of Texas hadn't even arrived on the scene.

The first substation was built north of Hugo, where Bill Grant's Bluegrass Festival is held now, according to Vance. "That first line ran through Nelson, Antlers, and on through Rattan, and it cost about $750 per mile." In 1998, the average cost was $26,400 per mile. The cost of line in 2010 is about $40,000 per mile.

With few employees in those early days, Vance's duties were many, and included everything from organizing town meetings for enlisting new members to negotiating for right-of-way easements.

"I was paid one hundred dollars a month—not bad money back then—and drove my own car," said Vance. He did a lot of driving up around the Smithville area. "On those mountain roads I was wearing out a full set of tires about every six weeks." In many of the areas where Vance would sign up new members, the roads were so poor that mule teams had to be used to haul in the utility poles.

Through the years, he watched the cooperative grow. "I didn't know land descriptions, but I had to learn pretty quick," he laughed. And Vance signed on new employees as he signed on new members.

Vance also helped to establish the current right-of-way agreements. "It wasn't always easy to get people to let us run lines across their place," he admitted.

Back then people didn't have electricity and didn't consider it a necessity as we do today. Some property owners weren't easily convinced of the benefits of allowing the lines onto their property.

"You might get one household signed up, and then have trouble getting the next property owner down the road okayed," said Vance. "The way the laws were set up back then, all utilities could use the section lines," he said. "So when we couldn't convince them to let us run line across a place, we would jag out to the section line and run it along to the property's edge. You can still see areas where it was done that way."

When World War II broke out, the co-op had to just wait it out, according to Vance. "We had contracts signed, but we couldn't get materials," he said. "Everyone was laid off—with the exception of one lineman, one office girl, and the manager—with the understanding that they would be rehired when the war ended."

Vance returned after the war to a new position—that of power use advisor. He served in that capacity for the next thirty-plus years until his retirement at the age of sixty-six.

I was born in 1939, and spent my youth in north McCurtain County, Oklahoma, in the area of Pickens, Oklahoma.

The area was comprised of small diversified farms where families raised everything they ate. Most food was prepared fresh. The only means of preservation was by canning everything possible, or by smoking/salting meat to help them get through the long, cold winter months. Of necessity, it was commonplace for each family to own a milk cow, hogs, chickens, and horses, which were essential to work the crops and for transportation.

Wood was the fuel for food preparation and for heating homes. Families' water supply was either drawn from a dug well or carried from a nearby spring, as my family did. Clothes were cleansed in wash pots heated by wood, using rub boards, rinsed by hand, and hung to dry on outside clotheslines even on the coldest of days. Women's hands would bleed due to exposure to harsh elements. Lamps and lanterns burning coal oil (kerosene) were used for lighting of homes, barns, churches, and schools. It was difficult to study and do homework in the evenings due to poor lighting provided by the one kerosene lamp at the kitchen table.

The Choctaw Lumber and Coal Company, which was later transformed into Weyerhaeuser Company, provided the main line of work in our area. Men and horses performed backbreaking, dangerous work in the timber from daylight to dark and some days before dawn. Then, after the long trip home, animals and evening chores had to be taken care of with a lantern in one hand (as had the morning chores). There were no electric appliances or tools of convenience. Electricity was a word not even thought of in our remote mountain area.

Excitement grew throughout the community the day Mr. Vance Womack contacted my father and explained the possibility of bringing electricity to our area. I was eleven years old and will never forget the day the survey crew came to our place and marked the line that would bring electricity to our home. Later, two men struggled for hours with the largest hand-held digger I have ever seen to pound a hole through the rocks. When the hole was finally dug to their satisfaction, a pole was set and wires connected us to another world.

Wires were stapled to the underside and across the ceiling in the house, and with the pull of a chain, each room in our three-room house filled with light; we received the miracle of electricity. It was a feeling beyond description to experience for the first time an entire room filled with light, reading a book, doing homework in any of the rooms I chose.

We received a monthly statement; it wasn't an electricity bill. We received a "light" bill. As time passed, the "light" bill became the "electricity" bill as appliances and other improvements were added to our home, barn, and shop.

My family has been with Choctaw Electric since that day long ago when it came to the Pickens area. Now, sixty years later, I feel blessed to still be reaping its benefits, thanks to our forefathers for their dedication and hard work in developing and organizing the Choctaw Electric Cooperative. We continue to be blessed by the dedicated leaders and employees of today who help keep Choctaw Electric Cooperative operating in an efficient, dependable manner.

Today, I cannot imagine life without electricity, and believe I appreciate it even more because I remember a time when it was not available. It is a necessity in today's society; it contributes to an easier lifestyle, and continues to give our rural communities access to the world.

Bob Holley
President, Choctaw Electric Board of Trustees

Every day...every meal...every farmer feeds this crowd

In 1960, every farmer will produce food aplenty for 25 people—27,375 square meals in all! This record productivity is now possible with the help of science, farmer know-how, chemicals, and *electric* power.

Yet, electricity, which has helped triple food production in only 25 years, was just a dream for most farmers as late as 1935. People, living in the country, were scattered . . . supposedly too costly to reach with light and power.

To get electricity, rural people organized into nonprofit local groups, borrowed money at interest from the REA and built their own lines. Today, nearly 1,000 locally-owned Rural Electric Systems operate 1½ million miles of line serving 16 million Americans.

As workers leave farms for other jobs, farmers are using more electricity to produce better food at lower cost. This means lower grocery bills for you and promises adequate food even when our population doubles in the years ahead.

Best of all, owner-users bear the cost of rural-electrification. Already they've paid more than $1 billion in principal and interest on their $3½ billion loans.

CHOCTAW ELECTRIC CO-OPerative
HUGO, OKLAHOMA
OWNED BY THOSE WE SERVE

Even as early as the 1940s, the co-op was working to help its members get the most for their electricity dollar. Vance helped members figure their heating and ductwork needs, recommending the proper equipment to update or install in new homes.

"I made it a point to establish friendships with the local contractors. Those friendships helped me to persuade them to build total electric homes, not a standard practice back then at that time," he said. "We also insisted that those new houses were insulated properly."

The many friendships formed by Vance while working at the co-op have endured, and citizens of Antlers—his home town—as well as the surrounding area always looked to him for advice and information about the co-op. He was always getting a wave or a friendly greeting. They may not have remembered Vance's name, but they recognized him as a Choctaw Electric employee.

Sam Smith began his career with CEC in 1956. After forty-one years with the company, Sam retired in 1998. For the majority of Sam's years with CEC, he served as area serviceman for members in Pushmataha County.

Whenever he was able to, Vance worked to promote the co-op. When Public Service of Oklahoma (PSO) expressed an interest in taking over Hochatown, he spoke to the people there, urging them to stay with Choctaw Electric. "I'm thoroughly sold on the co-op," he said. "I'm a satisfied customer!"

Yes, there is a lot that's new at Choctaw Electric in terms of expanded services and innovative ideas, but the standard of employee loyalty and providing quality service to our membership remain the same as when the cooperative was formed in 1940.

We at Choctaw Electric are proud to have people like Vance Womack and Ike Simpson on our side. As some of the earliest employees and members of Choctaw Electric Cooperative, they set a high standard that we are continuing to work hard to maintain in the tradition of affordable and dependable electrical service that was established from the very beginning.

CHAPTER SIX

FIRM POWER
is Essential

Choctaw Electric Cooperative had for many years received electricity from Public Service of Oklahoma (PSO) to provide to the co-op membership. About 1978 or 1979, PSO would no longer guarantee the rural co-ops "firm power," which is absolutely necessary. In order for co-ops to sustain an active membership, they must be able to depend on their electrical power source.

Choctaw Electric Cooperative, along with eighteen other rural co-ops in Oklahoma, jointly negotiated with Western Farmers Electric Cooperative (WFEC) to furnish the electrical needs of all of the co-ops with "firm power" agreements. So, in 1978–1979, WFEC started building the power plant located at the present site near Fort Towson. A 400-megawatt coal-fired generator was installed.

A Combined Cycle unit was put in operation at the Anadarko plant in 1977. It operates much like a turbofan jet engine on an airplane.

The Combined Cycle units are called that because they combine gas turbine and steam turbine power to turn the generator. First, natural gas is burned as fuel and the hot expanding exhaust is directed over the turbine blades, causing them to turn like a jet engine. The exhaust is then channeled into a small boiler and the heat creates steam that is piped into a steam turbine connected to the same generator as the gas turbine.

Hochatown Substation was built in the 1990s to lessen the loads of the Broken Bow and Bethel subs. Because our eastern service area has grown, this substation has proven to be an asset to Choctaw Electric members.

Western Farmers Electric Cooperative is a coal-fired generating plant located east of Hugo. Firm power agreements with WFEC have guaranteed a reliable and dependable source of power. *Photo courtesy of Mark Daugherty, WFEC.*

Blue Canyon Wind Farm, located on the Slick Hills terrain near the city of Lawton. Forty-five turbines generate wind power. WFEC purchased the wind farm's energy. *Photo courtesy of Mark Daugherty, WFEC.*

WFEC's Moreland plant began operation in March 1964. It is a conventional natural gas-fired boiler and steam turbine design. *Photo courtesy of Mark Daugherty, WFEC.*

> I've seen a lot of improvements and changes over the years. We have a lot less outages today and with new technology, we have a faster response time. Choctaw Electric Cooperative has a group of dedicated people working hard to help keep costs down, which is one of the biggest challenges we face today.
>
> Larry Johnson
> *Choctaw Electric Board of Trustees*

This method gets the maximum amount of work out of the fuel by using as much of the fuel's energy as possible. This is why the Combined Cycle units are WFEC's most efficient.

Each of the three Combined Cycle units is rated at over 134,000 horsepower and each weighs almost fifty tons. The units were built by General Electric and are housed in the newest part of the Anadarko plant, adjacent to the original plant.

These new units have attracted visitors from around the world to come see their efficiency firsthand. They added 300 megawatts to the plant's generating capacity, assuring plenty of electricity for the Choctaw Electric Cooperative membership's needs.

Water from the plant is taken from Fort Cobb Reservoir. About two million gallons of water is used in the boilers and treated with chlorine for use in the cooling towers.

Fuel for the plant is delivered by WFEC's natural gas pipeline system, which connects the plant to the rich gas-fields in western Oklahoma.

Choctaw Electric Cooperative has assured their membership that future electrical needs will be satisfied. Firm power agreements with Western Farmers Electric Cooperative have guaranteed a reliable and dependable source of power for the next seventy years and beyond.

We are keeping the lights on in southeast Oklahoma.

WFEC's Anadarko plant began generating electricity in 1953.
Photo courtesy of Mark Daugherty, WFEC.

CHAPTER SIX: FIRM POWER is Essential   57

CHAPTER SEVEN

Decade 2000
SEVENTY
Years of Progress

70 years
PEOPLE - POWER - PROGRESS

The beginning of the decade in 2000 started off with a lot of anxiety about the "Y2K Bug." We had been hyped by the media like never before, and we simply did not know what to expect when the new millennium arrived. Being a good steward, Choctaw Electric developed a plan to inform the public and to announce actions that would be undertaken to address the critical time period when the world would move from the twentieth century into the twenty-first century.

Given the co-op's growing use of digital devices and the impending Y2K event, CEC General Manager Johnie Grimes assembled a committee in early 1999 to compose a Y2K Contingency Plan. Grimes selected committee members from CEC operations, administrative, and member services departments in an effort to assess all aspects of the cooperative's operations and to draw upon a wide range of expertise.

Choctaw Electric Cooperative is not a generation and transmission entity, and therefore has no control over the supply of electricity to the distribution system. The committee concluded that the primary need was to prepare for the re-establishment of power to the distribution network and the problems that might be associated with it.

The plan detailed that all employees, as well as all key administrative and operations staff, including crewmen, would be on duty from 10 p.m. December 31, 1999, until 2 a.m. January 1, 2000.

Choctaw Electric personnel coordinated with local law enforcement personnel, emergency management agencies, and other community action agencies to inform them of the co-op's Y2K plan, as well as discuss general blackout and disaster preparedness.

Members of a Choctaw Electric area service crew, Larry Alford, Kyle Beck, Alan Billingsley, and Scotty Littles, install a pad mount transformer in the Beavers Bend area.

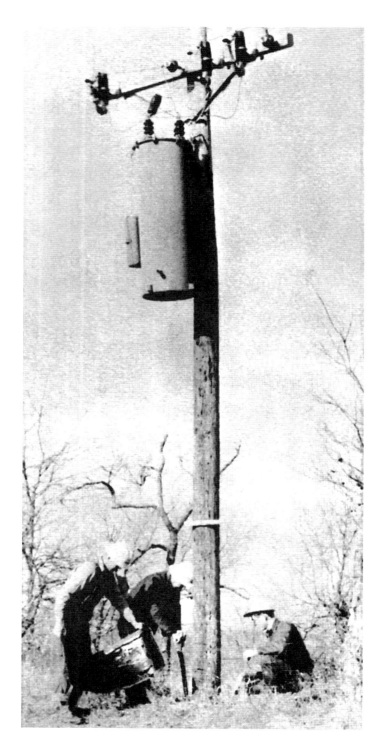
Choctaw Electric crews install and inspect an electric pole.

Choctaw Electric employee Jerrett Johnson upgrades service near Garvin, Oklahoma.

Area serviceman Guy Smith takes advantage of replacing a yard light using a bucket truck rather than the long-standing method by means of climbing gear.

Billy Holiday installs line equipment.

Choctaw Electric Cooperative distribution line near Golden, Oklahoma

Carter Mountain, located on Highway 259 north of Hochatown, is one of several towers that are jointly utilized for communication purposes.

Johnie Grimes, retired CEO of Choctaw Electric Cooperative

We happily welcomed in 2000 without a hitch, but we were prepared just in case something went awry. We were determined to start the decade of the 2000s with the lights still turned on in southeast Oklahoma.

Deregulation

One of the most significant happenings in co-op history was the implementation of deregulation in the state of Oklahoma. Following the Y2K experience, we began to focus on deregulating the electrical industry in the state, and discerning just how it would affect Choctaw Electric Cooperative.

And, because electric rates in Oklahoma are lower than most other states, our goal has been to keep them that way and to protect the interests of all consumers, particularly our membership in Choctaw Electric.

> The staff and employees at Choctaw Electric work in a professional manner. The co-op is working hard to keep rates as low as possible during these tough economic times. We are taking advantage of all the technology available to us, to help you, our member/consumer.
>
> Rodney Lovitt
> Choctaw Electric Board
> of Trustees

CHAPTER EIGHT

The
ICE STORMS
Testing Times

70 years
PEOPLE – POWER – PROGRESS

Freezing rain is certainly not uncommon in Oklahoma. Almost every winter storm that visits the state leaves a bit of ice as a calling card, along with the obligatory snow and sleet. Ice storms are a different story, however, especially those of the significant variety. They have struck throughout the state's recorded history, with varying degrees of damage.

The most damaging were the December 2000 winter storms that paralyzed southeast Oklahoma. A pre-winter ice storm began on December 13, 2000, and knocked out power to about 9,500 cooperative members located primarily in the southern and eastern service areas. Choctaw Electric crews and contractors worked around the clock and all repairs were completed in about a week. But the worst was yet to come. The force of nature struck again on Christmas Day in the form of a second ice storm. Because the damage was concentrated in the same areas that were hit hardest during the first storm, the sheer magnitude of this storm's destruction compared to the first one was the worst that southeastern Oklahomans had seen for several years.

Electric poles snapped one by one, and trees cracked and popped and came crashing to the ground from the sheer weight of the ice. Others were bent to the ground, bringing down utility poles and lines. Highways, rural roadways, and driveways were blocked by fallen limbs and downed power lines.

Road leading to Sobol communication tower. Many rural roads throughout the service area were blocked and impassable due to downed power lines and damaged poles, trees, and fallen limbs.

CHAPTER EIGHT: The ICE STORMS: Testing Times   67

CHAPTER NINE

Progressing Toward a Brighter Future

From the day that Choctaw Electric Cooperative was chartered, there has been growth and change. We came of age serving members who no one else wanted to serve because there was no wide margin of profit. Neighbors banded together to help each other by establishing their own avenue to modernization through electric power.

For the next thirty years, Choctaw Electric had to work hard to keep pace with the rapidly changing environment while looking to the future to meet the challenges of fast-paced changes.

The 1970s

The 1970s brought about multiple changes and challenges for the life of Choctaw Electric Cooperative. On December 29, 1972, the rural electric loan program was abolished by executive order. This meant that electric cooperatives could no longer borrow money for construction at 2 percent interest. A new program was established by Congress by which the cooperative could borrow a portion of their construction funds at 5 percent interest.

An energy crisis along with the cost of natural gas to generate wholesale power signaled an immediate change. In February 1977, for the first time in history, Choctaw Electric announced a rate increase that was equal to or cheaper than

Choctaw Electric Cooperative construction crews build new service for one of our members.

A 1970 poultry house proudly served by Choctaw Electric Cooperative

Choctaw Electric's first fleet of red service trucks became a familiar sight in rural southeast Oklahoma.

Choctaw Electric's current fleet includes advanced equipment that creates a safer, more efficient, and more productive environment for our servicemen.

any other cooperative in the U.S. To help our members meet these challenges, Choctaw Electric Cooperative directed educational and informational efforts toward conservation and energy efficiency.

Total electric homes and businesses were growing, security lights were being installed, and poultry growers were opting for total electric brooder houses.

Throughout Choctaw Electric's system, construction was taking place with the addition of equipment to existing facilities in order to keep pace with growth.

In 1974, the contract to purchase power from Southwestern Power Administration was ended and Western Farmers Electric Cooperative became our power supplier.

The 1980s

With the growing demand for electricity, supplies increased to meet rural American needs. It was during this decade that the power cost adjustment (PCA) was added to monthly bills, and members were introduced to peak alerts. Peak demands were costly and CEC members were encouraged to lower their electrical usage as much as possible from 4:00 p.m. until 8:00 p.m. from June through September to help lower the demand charge on the wholesale power bill.

The country made it through the energy crisis, but now it was facing a recession. Educational and informational efforts toward conservation and energy efficiency continued. Choctaw Electric Cooperative introduced the following new programs for its members:

- To help members cut down on usage, Choctaw Electric Cooperative introduced its Energy Audit Program.
- The Average Monthly Payment Plan was initiated to help members budget their utility bills.
- CEC Energy Efficient Loans were made available to members.

Although CEC members were still reading their own meters, a major change occurred in 1983 when in-house meter reading was initiated in the interest of revenue and billing accuracy.

The cooperative purchased its first in-house computer system during this time. All billing operations were converted over to the new system. The first computer billing statement received by Choctaw Electric members was issued on May 1, 1987.

The progression of wind power. *Photo courtesy of Mark Daugherty, WFEC.*

> When electricity became available to rural southeast Oklahoma seventy years ago it was hard to imagine all the ways it could be used. This was a significant and life-changing event for rural families. Today we serve more than seventeen thousand consumers in five counties and I have seen many significant improvements in service to the cooperative's membership over the fifteen years that I have served on the CEC Board of Trustees.
>
> Choctaw Electric is among the cooperative leaders using new technology. The old saying that "necessity is the mother of invention" holds true, especially in southeast Oklahoma. We can't predict every good thing that may happen in the future, but we can predict that consumers will always be taking advantage of the future through the use of this electric cooperative.
>
> Joe Brisco
> *Choctaw Electric Board of Trustees*

C. B. Rice, a dispatcher, tests new and modern radio equipment.

Veteran employee Larry Alford begins training on computerized equipment installed in service trucks allowing for faster response to outages, service calls, and day-to-day operations.

Matt Phillips, former Idabel district manager, was instrumental in securing some of the first key accounts and large loads for Choctaw Electric Cooperative. He was part of CEC for thirty years.

April 21, 1970

CHOCTAW ELECTRIC CO-OP
Meet The Friendly Ladies Who Serve You In The Choctaw Electric Office Seated Left To Right: Shirley Smith, Peggy Parker, Jan Cleveland And Winema Marbut. Standing Left To Right Willie Mae Nelms, Mickie Braudrick, Sharon Perry, Nettie Hendley And Mary Gilbreth. If You Have Any Questions Or Problems Concerning Electricity Give These Ladies A Call At 326-6486 And They Will Be Happy To Assist You

Choctaw Electric continued to press forward, securing large power contracts such as the Craig plant, Tyson Foods, Oklahoma Stone, and McCloud Correctional Facility. Matt Phillips, a former Choctaw Electric employee, was instrumental in promoting economic growth and development through these large power facilities.

The 1990s

Choctaw Electric progressed to the 1990s and celebrated fifty years of service to rural southeastern Oklahoma, at the time supplying power to over 12,280 members.

In 1991, the Board of Trustees approved a program to upgrade, replace, and add equipment and new construction throughout the system. The areas affected were Darwin, Unger, Broken Bow, Bethel, Holly Creek, Clayton, Nashoba, Mountain River, Westbank, Haworth, Rattan, Valliant, and Frogville. By making adequate upgrades, we were preparing for the future.

The Hochatown substation was built, lessening the load at both the Broken Bow and Bethel substations and allowing for more reliable service to our members.

January 1, 1998 marked the beginning of cycle billing for Choctaw Electric Cooperative. Cycle billing charges reflect the most recent month's usage. The old billing method had charged for electricity used two months prior to billing.

Choctaw Electric Cooperative continues to move forward to meet the demands of a highly technical world. Electric cooperatives are being redefined in order to keep pace with rapidly changing technology. Our commitment to you, our members, will not change. We will continue to provide quality electrical service at the lowest possible price.

Because there are electric cooperatives, today's rural America enjoys greatly diversified economic activity with greater stability and security for millions of its residents—a diversity that has reached into social and cultural life, enriching the community. And because there is electricity in rural America, there are choices in people's lives about where and how they live, with many finding rural America an attractive and desirable place to work and to raise families—still a land of opportunity.

CHAPTER TEN

TAKING
the Lead

70 years
PEOPLE – POWER – PROGRESS

In 2007, Choctaw Electric was awarded a U.S. Department of Agriculture Rural Development grant totaling $1.4 million. Partnering with Pine Cellular, the Community Connect grant funds were used to establish wireless broadband systems and community centers in Rattan, Haworth, and Smithville. Because Pine Cellular covers much of the same customer base area, this allowed us to share parts of our infrastructure for the broadband deployment.

Each community center was equipped with ten computers with high-speed Internet and free public access. For some of our members, this was the first time broadband had been made available. In addition, broadband service was provided to the local city police and volunteer fire departments, as well as various public schools.

"Choctaw Electric Cooperative exists, first and foremost, to serve the needs of our member-owners," said Terry Matlock, CEO of Choctaw Electric Cooperative. "Because it offers high capacity in a network that is simple to deploy and very economical to operate, we are able to bring our communities new and highly beneficial broadband service that has not been profitable for larger operators to provide."

Another program we have at Choctaw Electric emphasizes that we believe the single best way to improve our communities is to provide opportunities for our youth. That's why we invest annually in our area schools and have been long-time

An open house for the new community center in Rattan, one of three southeastern Oklahoma towns to benefit from a U.S. Department of Agriculture Rural Development grant through Choctaw Electric Cooperative. Choctaw Electric was awarded more than $1.4 million to establish wireless broadband systems in Smithville, Haworth, and Rattan.

Valliant Elementary School annually tours the CEC office in Hugo. Tours give students an opportunity to see the day-to-day operations of a distribution electric cooperative. Some hands-on opportunities are presented and electric safety education is always emphasized. Tours are available to all schools and organizations.

supporters of leadership organizations like 4-H, FFA, Boy Scouts, Girl Scouts, and many more similar programs.

There are unique opportunities available to students living in the Choctaw Electric service area. The annual Washington, D.C. Youth Tour is offered to high school juniors and the Oklahoma Youth Power Energy Camp is available to eighth-grade students.

Our call center is a centralized telephone-based service and support system located in the Hugo office. The call center uses a number of different technologies to help improve performance and customer experience. Call center technology evolves constantly, helping our call center representatives assist customers more efficiently and effectively.

We are proud of our safety program at Choctaw Electric. We participate in a National Accreditation Program, and our safety record is the envy of most other co-ops. We have steadily improved our safety record over the years to the point

The 2007 Youth Tour delegates. From left to right: Brian Wall, Megan Horn, Dustin White, Tasha Dale, Melinda Martin, and Justin Simpson. Youth Tour is a weeklong tour in our nation's capital, Washington, D.C. Choctaw Electric Cooperative sponsors delegates from schools in Choctaw, McCurtain, and Pushmataha counties. High school juniors are eligible for the trip.

Oklahoma Youth Power Energy Camp, now in its twenty-first year, has grown to more than seventy eighth-grade students participating each summer. Energy Camp develops leadership, friendship, and team-building. The camp is located at Red Rock Canyon near Hinton, Oklahoma. Students who wish to attend Energy Camp must enter a competition sponsored by Choctaw Electric Cooperative.

The earliest safety award was received in 1959–1960 for operating without an employee lost-time accident. CEC ranks nationally in the upper 98th percentile of all co-ops and we received a nationally recognized safety award in 2007 and 2009 for attaining the record that we are very proud to have received.

Choctaw Electric Cooperative received this award in June 2000 for working one million man-hours without a lost-time accident. CEC employees strive to create safe work practices and serve as a shining example for what can be achieved through cooperative efforts.

Sixth-grade students participate in a CEC Safety Program. Education programs are provided to all schools in our service area.

Darin Kirkes, CEC staking engineer, upgrades the system east of Idabel in the Redland area. Darin is using a transit, which is laser-type equipment that assists in working with the design of primary power line systems.

High voltage demonstration performed at Energy Camp, Hinton, Oklahoma.

of presently attaining over 1.5 million man-hours free of lost-time accidents.

We rank nationally in the upper 98th percentile of all co-ops and we received a nationally recognized safety award from the Rural Electric Safety Accreditation Program in 2007 and 2009 for attaining the record that we are very proud to have received.

Another issue we have addressed with a great deal of success is "service efficiency." A system-wide support program was implemented that allows case management of each telephone contact received at the co-op.

> As a former CEC lineman for fifteen years and now serving on the Board of Trustees since 1985, I have seen a lot of changes. Years ago we didn't use bucket trucks; instead, it was up and down electric poles the old-fashioned way, and some accidents occurred resulting in cuts and falls. We have modern equipment now and training and the focus on safety is important to us. CEC has one of the best employee safety records in Oklahoma.
>
> Bob Hodge
> *Vice-President, Choctaw Electric Board of Trustees*

Member telephone contacts are received at the dispatch-call center by call center personnel. The member's case record number will be followed throughout the system from the time the contact is initiated until the case is resolved. This process has greatly increased CEC customer support effectiveness as well as the response time to our membership.

The process of upgrading customer service required that we know the precise location of our nearly twenty thousand meters and four thousand miles of line. In 2008, an enormous mapping project took place, covering our complete distribution system that involved over one hundred thousand locations. The project was driven by a core desire to implement a staking system that could keep the global positioning satellite (GPS) system up to date on an ongoing basis.

Lacee Woodrum, Madison Cress, and Kara Johnson at Celebration Station in Oklahoma City while attending Youthpower Energy Camp.

The newly implemented GPS mapping system of our service area has given us the tools to respond to outages sooner, and has helped to advance our future system growth and customer service efforts.

A new innovative way to pay your electric bill was implemented in 2010. The e-bill service system allows members to pay their electric bill from home, work, or anywhere where there is a computer or telephone with Internet access, allowing for convenience and flexibility. Payments can be made twenty-four hours a day, seven days a week.

These are just a few of the benefits and improvements we at Choctaw Electric recently accomplished. We constantly strive to provide our members the best service at the most economical cost.

CHAPTER TEN: TAKING the Lead   89

CHAPTER ELEVEN

The CHOCTAW Electric Tradition

70 years

PEOPLE - POWER - PROGRESS

Choctaw Electric is a local business, owned by the people we serve. That means that we conduct business through a locally elected Board of Trustees and annual meetings where policy is proposed and voted on by consumers. It's the "people" part—the personal involvement and grassroots activities—that characterize what electric co-ops are all about.

We deliver service to you at the cost of service. There are no hidden fees and no profits for investors in faraway cities. Any money left over stays in our community and is put to work strengthening the economic wellbeing of our towns and neighborhoods.

Choctaw Electric Cooperative is a local business staffed by local professionals, so it is in a good position to listen and respond to your needs. All of these things that help consumers with energy conservation, economic development, and volunteerism point to one thing: Choctaw Electric and its staff are more than just an electric utility. We are an integral part of the community. That's why we will continue to do everything we can to improve the quality of life in your community. Because we are so closely linked to our communities, there are countless examples of activities that have "the co-op touch"—CEC conducts safety programs at schools and local libraries, sponsors county fairs and livestock shows, works with community organizations, and participates with civic groups.

Elliot Finley and Jacob Johnson inspect an oil circuit reclosure.

First, it is a pleasure to be serving on the Choctaw Electric Board of Trustees for almost a decade now. Watching the co-op continue to progressively evolve by the decisions we make at the board level, the CEO's level, and by the decisions every team member makes on a daily basis to make the co-op the best it can be is extremely rewarding, personally. I'm proud to know we are making a positive difference in the improved levels of service we strive to provide our customers, while doing it safely from the office to the field. The improvements, by all, are a true testament to the hard work every determined person at the co-op gives to ensure that our customers have continuous and reliable electric service whenever they desire.

I'm excited about the co-op's future as we continue to add improved and advanced technology to help the co-op operate more efficiently. These new technologies will continue to lessen outage times when they do occur and will help keep our people making repairs safer in the process. In today's rising energy consumption, demand, and raw materials costs, we will continue to work to keep the costs in check while being considered a consistently trusted electricity supplier to all we service. It's exciting times at Choctaw Electric. Again, I'm proud to be serving and happy to be playing a small role in the co-op's continued success.

Mike Bailey
Secretary, Choctaw Electric Board of Trustees

Choctaw Electric Cooperative is a company that cares about the people it serves. That service goes a long way beyond keeping the lights on: it's neighbors helping neighbors. That's what it's all about—that's the Choctaw Electric Cooperative tradition.

At Choctaw Electric Cooperative, one priority rings loud and clear: our members come first. Employees of CEC work hard to represent your interests—as members.

Electric cooperatives are "of, by, and for" the people we represent. Being a member of CEC means that you, along with your neighbors, own the company and have a voice in the decisions made on your behalf, and that is a fundamental difference between your local electric co-op and other energy providers.

The values CEC brings to the energy business keep us focused on serving your needs and your needs alone. Our "members first" focus ensures that we continually look for ways to improve our ability to meet your needs and to strengthen the quality of life in the communities in which we serve, live, and work. The trust

CEC crews upgrade service to the Tyson Food Plant located south of Broken Bow. Crews are upgrading this service while working on energized line; this allows the plant to continue with processing operations without interrupted electrical service.

Mechanic Donald "Rocky" Roxberry services a fleet vehicle. Choctaw Electric services and maintains the complete fleet of vehicles on-site.

Mike Wilkins, manager of electrical services, and Lisa O'Neill, system analyst, keep the communications infrastructure of CEC operating efficiently. This includes the CEC service area, CEC offices, and broadband sites.

Dale Smith, special equipment technician, programs TWACs meters to be read from the members' meters to the central office.

Billy Lampton, CEC dispatch coordinator, monitors and communicates radio traffic and the truck-tracking GPS system. Weather conditions are also observed and potential hazardous weather conditions are relayed to appropriate servicemen and crews in the hazard area.

you've placed in us is something we take very seriously, and work hard every day to earn.

Changes in the energy industry have certainly given others the opportunity to try and take advantage of our members, but CEC continues to fight every step of the way to ensure that the interests of every member we serve are protected—from the largest factory to the smallest business-owner on Main Street and to every one of the hardworking families that belong to the co-op.

But this is nothing new. Choctaw Electric Cooperative has been offering members a real choice from the day we opened our doors. Under the watchful eye of locally elected boards of trustees, America's nearly one thousand electric cooperatives are focused on delivering high-quality, reliable, and affordable service every day to the people and businesses we serve.

Our vision for the future is one that puts members first. This has been our commitment for seventy years and it will remain our commitment for years to come. The lights in southeast Oklahoma have been turned on and will only shine brighter in the future.

What are ELECTRIC Cooperatives?

Electric cooperatives are private, nonprofit corporations owned by the member-owners. They are similar in concept to other consumer-owned business like farm produce marketing co-ops. All cooperatives were formed using the "Rochdale Principles," a system designed by a group of weavers in Rochdale, England, to market their products.

The Rochdale Principles:

The Rochdale Principles that most member-owned cooperatives follow were originated by a band of weavers in Rochdale, England, in 1844.

- *Open Membership*: Those who may reasonably use the co-op's services—within the practical limits imposed by existing facilities, geography, etc.—must be permitted to join. None may be barred for such reason as race, religion, sex, nationality, or economic situation.
- *Democratic Control*: Effective means to control the organization must rest in the hands of the members on the basis of one member, one vote. In order to provide capital, members are urged to invest. No amount of investment, however, can earn more than one vote for any member.
- *Limited Return on Investment*: Dividends paid on invested dollars should provide a fair "rental" for the members' money, but a nominal ceiling on interest prevents speculation in co-op stock. Fundamentally, the cooperative exists to provide services to its members, not to return dollars for profit to investors.
- *Return of Margins to Members*: Dollars left over after all expenses would be regarded as profit for other organizations. In this case, however, they do not belong to the cooperative, but to the members and must be so allocated on the co-op books. Such dollars are returned to members, on a basis decided by the member-elected board, in proportion to each member's use of the service.

Any organization failing to measure up to any one of these four "principle" tests cannot be considered a cooperative. Beyond these, the International Cooperative Alliance believes two more practices to be so essential to cooperative success that it has proclaimed them to be principles also. They are:

- *Continuing Education*
- *Cooperation Among Cooperatives*

Each consumer of the cooperative is a member, with one vote in the affairs of the cooperative. Members adopt bylaws and lay out guidelines to assure a democratic organization. Directors who serve on the Board of Trustees are elected by members at an annual members meeting.

Rates are established by the local cooperative Board, based upon what it actually costs to provide dependable electric service. Rates are designed so that revenues exceed expenses. The "margin" is then allocated back to members of the cooperative in the form of capital credits. Members receive money back based on the amount of electricity they have used during the allocation period. The return of capital maintains the non-profit status of the cooperative.

Electric Cooperatives are Different from Investor-Owned Utilities

Electric cooperatives are private, independent electric utilities, owned by the members they serve. As democratically governed businesses, electric cooperatives are organized under the Cooperative or Rochdale Principles, anchoring them firmly in the communities they serve and ensuring that they are closely regulated by their consumers.

Members of electric cooperatives express higher than average levels of customer satisfaction. It's no wonder. Electric cooperatives are different than other forms of business, and member-owners of cooperatives notice this difference. For one thing, co-ops put consumers first because the consumers are the owners. In addition, co-ops are locally owned and operated. When members call the co-op, they are talking with their neighbors. And both of these aspects combine to make co-ops more responsive since members are the owners and they are accountable to their own neighbors and communities.

An investor-owned utility (IOU) is owned by stockholders who may or may not be customers and who may or may not live in the service area. The IOU is a for-profit enterprise. Stockholders have as many votes in elections as the number of shares he or she owns. Those who own the most shares control the corporation. Business decisions and matters of policy are decided by the Board of Directors and officers who are elected by stockholders. Net margins are either divided among the stockholders on the basis of the amount of stock owned or used to expand business. The Board of Directors decides how net margins will be used.

Electric Cooperative Acronyms & Definitions

ACRE   Action Committee for Rural Electrification

CEC   Choctaw Electric Cooperative

CFC   Cooperative Finance Corporation

CFL   Compact Fluorescent Light

Distribution Cooperative   Purchases power at wholesale from a Generation and Transmission (G&T) cooperative and delivers it at cost to members

G&T   Generation and Transmission cooperative, owned by several distribution cooperatives to furnish their own generating plants and transmission lines to supply power to their member cooperatives

IOU   Investor-Owned Utility

kw   Kilowatt

KWH   Kilowatt Hour

NRECA National Rural Electric Cooperative Association

OAEC   Oklahoma Association of Electric Cooperatives

PCA   Power Cost Adjustment

REA   Rural Electrification Administration, a lending agency with the U.S. Department of Agriculture

REC   Rural Electric Cooperative

RUS   Rural Utility Service

SURE   Speak Up for Rural Electrification, a political action committee for electric cooperatives

TVA   Tennessee Valley Authority

USDA   United States Department of Agriculture

WFEC   Western Farmers Electric Cooperative

Rural Electrification Organizational Chart

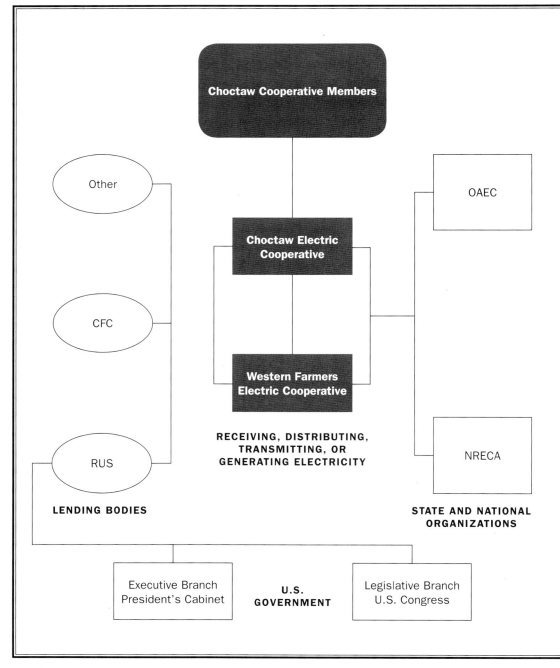

Business Types Compared

FEATURES	INVESTOR-OWNED	MEMBER-OWNER
Who owns the business?	The stockholder	The member-owner
Who uses the services?	Generally non-owner customers	Member-owner
Who votes?	Common stockholders	Member-owner
How is the voting done?	By shares of common stock	One member-owner, one vote
Who determines policies?	Common stockholders	Member-owners
Are returns on ownership capital limited?	No	Yes, usually 8% or less
Who gets the net margins?	The stockholders, in proportion to the number of shares of stock owned	The member-owner, based upon the amount of business done with the cooperative

Choctaw
Electric Cooperative
1940–2010

Board Managers

P. R. Higgins

Jack Granbrell

Jess Ogden

Leon Bates

Carl Gayle

Robert Mace

Mickie Braudrick

Johnie Grimes

Terry Matlock

Board Members, Past & Present

John A. Bryan	1940–1950
S. M. Dancer	1940–1942
Ray Grant	1940–1977
Jim Miller	1940–1941
Paul Mollenkopf	1940–1957
Enoch Needham	1940–1942
B. E. Nobles	1940–1952
Virgil Jumper	1941–1954
E. E. Bussell	1942–1948
Vance Womack	1942–1949
A. A. Boren	1948–1964
Newman Helm	1948–1963
E. G. Wilson	1948–1982
J. M. Goin	1950–1976
Clarence Adams	1952–1975
Jeff Weathers	1954–1968
John Mollenkopf	1957–1976
Leonard Sherrer	1963–1982
Leonard Wooten	1965–1978
Barney Ward, Jr.	1968–1982
Charles Rhodes	1975–1978
Emmit E. Henderson	1976–1982
Elvin Morris	1976–1982
Bill Grant	1977–1982
R. W. May	1978–1982
Curry Scott	1978–1982
Roger Armstrong	1982–1983
Bill Easterwood	1982–1994
Jerry Ellis	1982–1984

W. M. "Bill" Houchen	1982–1985
Cliff House	1982–1984
C. A. "Bud" Jackson	1982–1989
Wilbur Lee	1982–1984
Karen Spradling	1982–1984
J. C. Wallace	1982–1984
Irma Burkham	1984–1986
Haskell Willingham	1984–1985
Joann Zoppe	1984–1990
Grant Wilson	1984–1987
Buddy Anderson	1985–present
Cecil Butler	1985–1987
Leoma Caldwell	1986–1989
Lela Campbell	1986–1994
Joey Hairrell	1986–1995
Carl Boykin	1987–1992
Gale Smith	1987–1992
Danny Antwine	1989–1998
L. K. Johnson	1989–2002
Bill McCain	1989–present
Glenn Cox	1993–1996
Bob Hodge	1993–present
Henry Baze	1994–present
Joe Brisco	1994–present
Jean Lovitt	1995–2006
Bob Holley	1998–present
Mike Bailey	2001–present
Larry Johnson	2002–present
Rodney Lovitt	2007–present

Employees, Past & Present

Many hours were spent searching through the archives for past Choctaw Electric Cooperative employees. Every effort has been made to gather a complete list of employees and ensure the accuracy of each employee name. Numerous archived typewritten documents were gone through; names that were gathered from the past are printed as they were recorded in these records. We apologize if anyone has been omitted from this list.

As you see a familiar name, whether it is a friend or a family member, no doubt it will stir reminders of personal stories, pleasant memories, and remembrances of that person. We hope the employees' names that appear here will serve as a reminder of Choctaw Electric's past and as a vision of the future.

Chandy Abney
Hubert G. Adams
Otho Arthur Adams
Jimmie K. Ainsworth
Brian Akard
Marion Albertson
Larry Alford
Lloyd Allen
Raymond Allen
Tonia Allred
Kurren G. Anderson
Steve Anderson
Walter Lee Andrews
Joseph "Taco" Antu
Robbie Fern Antwine
Deana Armes
Vernon D. Aulgur
Vesta Maxine Awbrey
Mary Babcock-Gilbreth
J. B. Bailey
Byron R. Baker
Derek Baker
Sybil Barber
Darryl Barnes
C. S. Barrick
Bill Barton
Le Roy Baskin
H. F. Bass
Leon Bates
Frank Bear
Kathy Beasley
Lois Ann Beason
Kyle Beck
Bernie Bell

Doyle Bell, Jr.
Allen Billingsley
D. E. Billingsley
George Billingsley
Jeremy Billingsley
G. M. Bingham
Ronnie Bishop
A. J. Blacksher
E. W. Bloodworth
Orren Jean Bloodworth
Robert Harold Bocoy
Jennifer Boling
Gladys Esther Bond
Robert E. Bone
Doyle Bostic
Leonard Bowen
John Box
Claude Bracken
Vernon Braddy
Lesley K. Brannon
Lee Roy Branton
John W. Braudrick
Cecil Bray
Terry Joe Brents
Willis H. Brents
Carl Brewer
Debbie Brock
Alvin F. Brown
C. G. Brown
Charles Richard Brown
Lynn I. Browning
Lori Bryan
Anita Bryant
H. B. Bryant

Merle Bryant
Karri Buchanan
C. F. Burchfield
Ford Burchfield
James Burchfield
Harrison Burnett
James M. Bush
R. W. Butler
C. L. Byrd
Harris Edwin Calaway
A. L. Calfee
Emmett Campbell
Rufus N. Carley
Chrystal Carper
Balleid L. Carterby
Doug Carvan
G. H. Carver
Harold E. Casey
Lloyd Cather
Pat Chaffin
Walter Chambers
Howard B. Chancey
Debbie Childers
Elmer Christian
Winford Clardy
James A. Clark
Haskell E. Clifton
J. J. Cline
Francis Clinkenbeard
Larry Cody
Edward Coffman
Tammie Coleman
John Colfax
Roy Colley

Wilburn B. Colley
Ray Collins
Marshal Compton
Mose Compton
Jim Oliver Cook
Karen Cooper
Ken Cooper
Quarter Main Cooper
Crystal Copeland
Dewayne Courtwright
James E. Courtwright
Johnie J. Courtwright
Howard Lon Cousins
Samuel Credell
Tommy Joe Crowder
Buster Croy
Guy Dale
Karan M. Daniels
Marcia Davee
Harold Davis
Jackie Davis
Kenneth R. Davis
Leonard Decker
Bobby J. Degman-Snow
Dawn Demarra
L. F. DeShazo
Jack Dickerson
Tom Dickerson
Gerald O. Disney
Margery Divine
James Dollarhide
Dwight Donica
Joe Douglas
Cullie Clovis Doyle
Winfield Doyle
John E. Drake
Richard L. Draper
Linda Dyer
Bill Easterwood
Ervin Eaves
Glenna Jean Edge
J. C. Ellis
Lorie Ellis
Mickie Elmore-Braudrick
David England
Mamie Lee Epperson
Amos Erwin
Brad Farley
L. A. Farmer
Amos H. Farrar
Rudolph Farrar
Elliot Fenley
Jim Ferguson

Francis Ferrier
Clifton Dale Fields
Billy Don Flanagan
Stanley Flannagan
Gene Floyd
Haskell Floyd
Bud Fly
Roy Lee Fort
C. E. Foster
C. F. Foster
Ron Frandsen
Antoinette Frazier
Darren Frazier
Tobias W. Frazier, Jr.
Bobby Freeman
Lynn Freeman
Rita Freeman
Harvey Friend
Walter E. Friend
Willie Friend
Lewis Frye
Omar Fugate
Louis Gammon
Ruby Gann
Billy N. Gardner
Jim Gardner
Lyman Garman
Dean Garrison
Carl Gayle
Henry L. German
Roscoe Gilbert
Bin Gilliam
A. J. Glass
Chris Goeken
Raymond Lee Golden
Warren George Goodlow
Harold J. Grace
Howard J. Grace
Jack Granbrell
Alta Mae Gray
Joseph Gray
Lucille Green
Sherlene Green
Curtis L. Griffin
Helen Griffin-Angelly
Johnie Grimes
Roy G. Guin
N. W. Hadley
Adam Halcomb
Junior E. Hall
Hozell Halloway
Tony Hallows
Bill Hammons

J. W. Hammons
Krystle Hampton
Jess Handley
Sam Hanes
Charles R. Harley
Farney Harmon
John F. Harmon
Billy L. Harper
F. M. Harrison
Sam Harrison
Elmer Harry
Bob Hartman
Roy E. Hartman
Hirace L. Hatton
R. C. Hawkins
Russell Haynes
Pauline Hayslip
Darrel Heath
Oscar Hedge
Nettie Hendley
Shonda Hendon
Edward Earl Hendricks
Melissa Herman
P. R. Higgins
Marion Hill
Steven Hilton
Elmer Hinsley
Coy Hinton
Ollie Hobbs
Mica Holbrook
Howard B. Holder
Billy Holiday
Joyce W. Holiman
Troy Holloway
J. C. Holman
Raymond Holman
R. V. Hooks
Allen Horn
Hank Horn
Harmon Hornbeck
James R. Horton
John Houchen
Sid House
Carl Hughes
Raymond Humphrey
Ruth Pearl Hunkapiller
Dan Hunter
W. Don Hunter
James Hurlburt
Charlie Clifton Ingram
Bennie L. Jackson
Jerry Jackson
Amanda Janoe

Mary Jasper
Anderson Jeffery
Fred Jenkins
Louie Jenkins
Cornelius John
Albert Johnson
Clyde Johnson
Henry Johnson
Jacob Johnson
Jerret Johnson
Jia Johnson
Toby Johnson
W. C. Johnson
Willie H. Johnson
C. W. Jones
Robert M. Jones
Sam Paul Jones
Sue Jones
Johnnie F. Jordan
Eugene Keeling
Brad Kendrick
Lewis Kimmell
Tomye D. Herren
Terry Kinslow
Darin Kirkes
Patricia Ann Kitchen
David Knight
Edgar Knox
Jimmie Wayne Knox
Mike Knox
Samuel Thomas Knox
Lonzo Lamb
Roy H. Lambert
Billy Lampton
Crystal Langley
George R. Lankford
Joe E. Laster
Deana Lawless
Marty A. Lawless
Clint Leathers
John Troy Lee
B. J. LeForce
Beatrice Lentz
Joe E. Lentz
LaVerne Lindly
Karen Lindly
Scotty Littles
Lloyd Glen Long
Brian Louderback
Bernice Loveless
Carl Lowe
Trine Lucas
Pam Luna

Freeman Lynn
Raymond P. Lynn
Robert Mace
Loy Lee Madding
Mike Maggby
Joe E. Mahaffey
Mike Mahaffey
Jimmy Malone
Maxie Mann
Winema Marbut
Derek Martin
Terry Matlock
John Anderson Matthews
Janet Maynard
Benjamin Maytable
Bennie Benson Maytable
John Quincy Maytable
R. D. McCalman
Nancy McCarty
Diane McCary
Aaron McClure
Freeman McClure
Noel McClure
Robert S. McCommans
John McCormick
Tom McCurry
Hiram McDonel
John D. McGovern
James McKenzie
R. V. McKinney
W. R. McKnight
A. C. McLead
Ivy McVay
Jimmy H. Menefee
O. L. Milam
Jeremy Miller
Randy Mills
Edgar Mitchell
H. H. Momaw
George Monday
Leslie Moore
Martha Andrien Moore
Henry D. Moorman
Josh Morgan
Edwin Morris
Elvin Morris
George F. Morris
W. A. Morris
Clayton Morse
William Murray
Buford Nabors
W. D. Narramore
Carroll Needham

H. E. Needham
Cecil I. Neely
Harry H. Nelms
Sylvia Ramona Nelms
T. H. Nelms
Willie Mae Nelms
Jim Nelson
John T. Newman
Terry Noel
David Nowabbie
Lisa A. O'Neill
James Oakes
Jess Ogden
Phil Orr
Wallace Blake Palmer
Therman Parish
Bill Parker
D. L. Parker
G. L. Parker
Silas Harvey Parker
William B. Parker
James R. Parnell
Robert Parnell
Joyce Arlene Partin
Stacy Partin
Kaleb Payne
Reuge Pelt
R. Dean Pennon
Tom L. Pennon
Joe Penson
John Houston Perry
Marcus Peters
Tommy Joe Peterson
Dale Pettyjohn
Milas Ervin Pfaff
Ricky Pfaff
Sandra Pharis
Brad Phillips
Jake Phillips
Matt Phillips
J. A. Phinney
Monte Pitt
Allene Pogue
Odell H. Popchoke
Hilary Pound
Joe Taylor Powell
L. V. Powers
Joseph A. Prince
Jill Randell
Vance Raulston
Bailee Ray
Rex Coleman Ray
Jeff Rector

Johnnie Rector
Dale Redwine
Keith Reed
Luther Reynolds
Elton Rhodes
Mary Jane Rhodes
J. E. Rice
James Richard
Joe Nathien Richard
Berry Roan, Jr.
Melba Roan
Tré Roberts
G. L. Robertson
Dale Roden
D. O. Rodenberger
Thomas L. Rorie
George T. Rosenthal
Johnnie R. Rosenthal
Donald "Rocky" Roxberry
Gwendolyn Ruffin
Kobi Russ
Mary Ann Rymel
Hershey Sanders
Leonard Sanders
Kay Sattawhite
James D. Satterfield
Curry Scott
Victor E. Scott
Brian Scroggins
Hershel L. Sharp
Ruth Jean Shelton
L. M. Shepard
Lee Shields
Mathu Shoals
Jodie Simmons
Bernice G. Simpson
Harry H. Simpson
Hershel Simpson
Isaac J. Simpson
Willis Lee Sims
Ione Slaton
Billy W. Smith
Billye Smith
Dale Smith
George E. Smith
George S. Smith
Guy Smith
Isaac Smith
James Kenneth Smith
Kendra Smith
Nancy Smith
Sam Smith
Sam B. Smith, Jr.

Shirley Smith
Sheree Snyder
Henry Dewey Sorrell
Dale Standifer
Richard L. Standridge
George Stanfield
Dean Stapleton
Leroy Stebar
Evert Stephenson
Wanda Stevenson
Steven Stewart
James Storie
Frank Stout
Sam Stout
George Strawn
Jimmy H. Stuart
Cary E. Sweet
A. V. Tarkington
B. D. Taylor
Charles Taylor
Edward Earl Taylor
Jerry Taylor
Milton Taylor
Bill Teague
Bart Tedder
Gordon Thomas
L. O. Thomas
Mack Thomas
Hershel L. Thompson
Michael Thompson
Orvel J. Thurman
Charles Edward Toliver
Amos J. Tramble
Prentis Tramble
Barbara Tullos
Marques Turbyfill
Lloyd Turnage
Max Turner
Ross Turner
O. L. Upton
Jody Usery
Roger Vandever
Clyde Wadley
A. V. Waldrup
Ice Walker
Norman Walker
Pertie Walker
Pam Wall
Susan Wall
H. W. Wallis
Mabel Brown Walton
Anderson Ward
Darrell Ward

R. L. Ward
Truman C. Ward
Woodrow Ward
Twana Ware
Dorothy May Warren
Lonnie Leroy Washington
Leo Allen Watson
R. C. Watson
Theo Allen Watson
Harold Watts
Randy Watts
Mary Ann Webb
Paula Welch
Jackey Wells
Tippett Wells
James West
Virgil West
Harold Dale Whala
Steve Wilhelm, Jr.
Melvin Wilkins
Michael Wilkins
Bois Williams
Joe Williams, Jr.
L. E. Williams
Paul Williams
R. M. Williams
Ray Williams
Tommie Williams
M. L. Williamson
William J. Williston
Jimmy Winship
Renea Winters
Frank Wolf
James M. Wolfe
Vance Womack
Bob Wood
Seth Wood
Wyatt Wood
Bernard L. Woodman
Charlie Woodrum
Earl Woodrum
Jack Wooldridge
L. L. Woolsey
R. L. Woolsey
Floyd Wright
George Wright
Letha Wright
Vernon Wright
William E. Wright
David Young
Tim Young
Mark Zachry

About the Author

Herb Matlock resides in Garvin, Oklahoma. He has been married to Mary Jo (McPhail) Matlock for sixty years. He and Mary Jo have four sons, five grandchildren, and three great-grandchildren. Mr. Matlock attended Southeastern Oklahoma State University, Oklahoma City University, and the University of Oklahoma.

Mr. Matlock served for four years in the United States Air Force. He and his family moved from Oklahoma to France and resided in Europe for two years, where he participated in the management of the Jet Engine Overhaul Program for NATO countries. He is retired from the Federal Aviation Administration and from the Kiamichi Economic Development District of Oklahoma.

Mr. Matlock is former chairman of the Southeast Oklahoma Work Force Investment Board, former president of the Oklahoma State Association of Work Force Investment Board, former mayor of Garvin, and was the publisher of the *Valliant Challenger* newspaper. He has also served three different Oklahoma state governors as an appointed member of their boards or commissions.

Most recently, Mr. Matlock served as a member of the Oklahoma governor's Council for Work Force and Economic Development and was a Foundation trustee of the E. T. Dunlap Higher Education Center. He currently serves as the chairman of the Little Dixie Community Action Agency. He is also a rancher and is the owner of an independent consulting business.